UNLESS THE
LORD
BUILDS THE HOUSE

LIVING AN EXTRAORDINARY LIFE IN GOD

HAMP LEE III

(com)mission™
PUBLISHING

MONTGOMERY, ALABAMA

Unless the Lord Builds the House: Living an Extraordinary Life in God / Hamp Lee III. 1st ed.

Library of Congress Control Number: 2017949242
ISBN: 978-1-940042-60-2

CONTENTS

Except the Lord build the house, they labour in vain that build it: except the Lord keep the city, the watchman waketh but in vain.
PSALM 127:1

INTRODUCTION

From our earliest moments growing up, we learned to dream. We wanted to be a doctor, lawyer, race car driver, or the president. No borders existed on what could be possible for us. And between right now and someday, we looked for our dreams to become a reality.

But along the path of life, certain events and circumstances brought on discouragement, anger, and frustration. Our once limitless possibilities became limited. We only wanted a small slice of happiness for ourselves. But instead of a slice of happiness, we received a pound of persecution, trials, and tribulation.

Through the darkness that sometimes comes in life, there is a ray of hope. Hope comes through God and His promises. And in spite of our discouragement, anger, and frustration, God stayed with us just as He said.[1] Even when we were unfaithful, He was there to lift our heads, encourage our hearts, and remain an ever-present help in our time of need.[2]

Reading through the bible, we witness God's people face many challenges, opposition, and persecution. And time and again, God came through for them...*right on time.*

As a child of God, you might be looking for God to come through for you. You hope God will be right on time to help you in the midst of your situations. You want Him to bless you, lift you, promote you, and bring you peace. *And why not?!* You are His child, and He loves you. You have gone through so much in your life, and with God on your side, things should be getting better. You should be back on track, seeing your dreams and goals realized, and becoming the person you set out to become...*or should you?*

I wrote *Unless the Lord Builds the House: Living an Extraordinary Life in God* to describe the life you can live between now and someday. Even within the trials and tribulation you might experience on a daily basis, there is something wonderful happening within you. God has an extraordinary life for you to live before Him and His children. And it is my prayer that

---

[1] Hebrews 13:5.

[2] Psalm 46:1–3.

you will come to see the beauty of your life as God unfolds it before you.

CRIBS HOUSE

In 2000, MTV aired a reality show called MTV Cribs. MTV Cribs displayed the houses of celebrities, musicians, actors, and athletes. It was an inside look into how these individuals lived and spent their money on houses, cars, clothes, and other things.

From then on, anytime I saw a big house, I referred to it as a *cribs house*. Now, I did not see anything wrong with owning a *cribs house*. It was a part of my own *American Dream*—to own a big house where I could relax, have a bit of room, and live in luxury.

But when you think about it, we might all want a *cribs house*. A *cribs house* could represent dreams and goals, such as a husband or wife, children, a particular career, vacations, and all manner of accolades, opportunities, and successes. You might plan and work really hard to make your *cribs house* a reality...and then one day you meet God.

One encounter with God can change a person's life forever...

Abraham

Abram was living in Haran with his family when God called him.[3] God told him to go to a land He would show him later.

Abram departed with his wife, his nephew, and all the things they had into the land of Canaan. God would later change his name from Abram (high father) to Abraham (father of a multitude) as he would become the father of many nations.[4] All nations of the earth would be blessed through him.[5] God would make a covenant with Abraham to give his future generations the land from the river of Egypt to the Euphrates river.[6]

Gideon

Gideon was in the least significant family in the tribe of Manasseh and he was the youngest (smallest) in his father's house. But God called him to take three hundred men into battle against an army of at least one hundred thirty-five thousand soldiers.[7] Through God, Gideon won a decisive victory, delivering the

---

[3] Genesis 12:1–3.

[4] Genesis 17:5–9.

[5] Genesis 12:2, 22:15–18

[6] Genesis 15:15-18.

[7] Judges 8:10.

entire people of Israel from their enemies and giving them forty years of peace.[8]

Mary

Being engaged to Joseph, Mary might have considered a happy existence in marriage, with children and a good home. But one day God sent the angel Gabriel to Mary to tell her that she found favor with God. She would conceive and give birth to the Son of God![9]

When Mary was found to be pregnant (it did not seem she told Joseph of the circumstances of her pregnancy), he sought to divorce her quietly.[10] But before he could divorce her, an angel of the Lord appeared to him and told him Mary's conception was from the Holy Spirit:

Joseph, thou son of David, fear not to take unto thee Mary thy wife: for that which is conceived in her is of the Holy Ghost. And she shall bring forth a son, and thou shalt call his name JESUS: for he shall save his people from their sins. Now all this was done, that it might be fulfilled which was spoken of the Lord by the prophet, saying, Behold, a virgin shall be with child, and shall bring forth a son, and they shall call his

[8] Judges 8:28.

[9] Luke 1:26–38.

[10] Matthew 1:19.

name Emmanuel, which being interpreted is, God with us.[11]

Joseph awoke from his sleep and took Mary as his wife. When she gave birth to her firstborn son, he called His name Jesus.[12]

When many of us encounter God, we do expect our lives to change. Many of us think about how God can improve our lives. We consider how He can help us get our *cribs house* and accomplish our dreams and goals.

This is our expectation, but at the time, we might not consider whether what we hope for is the same as what God plans for us. Now, I do not believe there is anything wrong with having dreams and goals. But we must all understand that those dreams and goals might not be the same as the plan and purpose God has for us.

A man's heart deviseth his way: but the Lord directeth his steps.[13]

Reflection

Describe your initial encounter with God.

----

[11] Matthew 1:20–23.

[12] Matthew 1:24–25.

[13] Proverbs 16:9.

What are your current dreams and goals?

Did you ever expect God to help you accomplish your dreams and goals? If yes, please explain.

If your dreams and goals were not accomplished within a specific timeframe or delayed longer than you expected, were you ever discouraged, angry, or frustrated with God or others? If yes, please explain.

JAILHOUSE

God called Jonah to go to Nineveh and cry out against the city.[14] Jonah knew God was gracious, merciful, slow to anger, of great kindness, and repents of evil.[15] He knew if the people repented of their conduct and turned from their evil ways, God would repent of the evil He said He would do to them through his warning.[16] But this was not what Jonah wanted for Nineveh. So instead of going to Nineveh, he headed in the opposite direction toward Tarshish.[17]

As our lives unfold before God, our encounters with Him might not bring the happiness and success

---

[14] Jonah 1:1.

[15] Jonah 4:2.

[16] Jonah 3:9–10.

[17] Jonah 1:2.

we expected for ourselves. What we imagined, desired, and hoped for might not come as fast as we would like. Many of us might become angry, bitter, and disobedient. We often move in the opposite direction like Jonah. We refuse to do what God asked of us because it is not what we wanted for ourselves or others.

We wanted God's help in getting our *cribs house*. But many of us feel like we are in the jailhouse— unable to do the things we want to do, live how we want to live, and receive the things we want, so we go our own way. We become determined to make our dreams and goals a reality.

When Jonah traveled his own way, he and others around him experienced great tribulation. As he traveled on a ship going to Tarshish, the Lord sent a great wind into the sea, and there was a mighty tempest. The winds were so strong that the shipped seemed that it would break apart.[18] The mariners were afraid, and each cried out to their god. They even threw their cargo overboard to lighten the ship.[19] But Jonah was fast asleep in the innermost part of the ship.

When we choose to go our own way, those around us are affected as well. The mariners with Jonah lost their cargo and were afraid that they might

---

[18] Jonah 1:4.

[19] Jonah 1:5.

lose their lives. But Jonah was unaware of the destruction his actions were causing. He was fast asleep. The same might be occurring with you.

When you are discouraged, angry, and frustrated with the life you are living (or God wants you to live), you might not *see* how your actions affect others. You can only see how *life* is not going the way you would like. You might be *fast asleep* to what is going on around you until you get what you want or someone or something gets your attention.

Reflection

If known, describe the plan and purpose God has provided for your life.

Are the purpose and plan God has for you different from what you imagined for your life? If yes, please explain.

How has God's plan and purpose for your life affected your previous goals and plans?

Have you been unwilling to accept the plan and purpose God gave you? If yes, please explain how.

FORECLOSURES

A foreclosure is the action of taking possession of a mortgaged property when the mortgagor fails to keep up their mortgage payments. When you think of a foreclosed house, you might think of a run-down property with an unkempt yard, curtains hanging off the windows, and all types of stuff sprawled throughout the house. It is a visual representation of someone who no longer cares about the property.

When Jonah failed to follow through on the word of the Lord, he and the ship's crew was in danger of losing everything, including their lives. When the mariners learned Jonah was causing their current distress, he told them to throw him overboard to save themselves.[20] Though they were initially reluctant

---

[20] Jonah 1:6–15.

and terrified, they cast Jonah into the sea, and the seas stopped her raging.[21]

In many ways, Jonah's life was in foreclosure. He had an opportunity to build a life by God's design and instead, chose his own path.

The Lord had a great fish to swallow Jonah. He spent three days and three nights in its belly. It gave Jonah time to reflect on the course of his life and his actions leading up to the fish swallowing him. While in the fish's belly, Jonah said a prayer to the Lord:

I cried by reason of mine affliction unto the Lord, and he heard me; out of the belly of hell cried I, and thou heardest my voice. For thou hadst cast me into the deep, in the midst of the seas; and the floods compassed me about: all thy billows and thy waves passed over me. Then I said, I am cast out of thy sight; yet I will look again toward thy holy temple. The waters compassed me about, even to the soul: the depth closed me round about, the weeds were wrapped about my head. I went down to the bottoms of the mountains; the earth with her bars was about me for ever: yet hast thou brought up my life from corruption, O Lord my God. When my soul fainted within me I remembered the Lord: and my prayer came in unto thee, into thine holy temple. They that observe lying vanities forsake their own mercy. But I will sacrifice unto thee with the

---

[21] Jonah 1:15.

voice of thanksgiving; I will pay that that I have vowed. Salvation is of the Lord.[22]

When Jonah finished his prayer, the Lord spoke to the fish, and it vomited him out upon the dry land.[23]

When we live in disobedience to God, many of us experience the destruction of our actions firsthand. But sadly, some people are so discouraged, angry, and frustrated that they never realize it or it takes many years before they do—losing many relationships and opportunities along the way.[24] But when we find ourselves in such situations, I pray we will have a moment of reflection like Jonah.

Some people will only listen to God after they have reached the very bottom of their situation and experienced extreme loss. Only in the darkness and loneliness of their lives will they reach out to God. But praise God when they heed His call!

For godly sorrow worketh repentance to salvation not to be repented of: but the sorrow of the world worketh death.[25]

---

[22] Jonah 2:2–9.

[23] Jonah 2:10.

[24] Proverbs 16:18.

[25] 2 Corinthians 7:10.

Jonah received another opportunity to fulfill the word of the Lord given to him. After being vomited out by the fish, the Lord told him a second time to go to Ninevah and preach against it. Jonah arose and traveled directly to Ninevah according to the word of the Lord.[26]

Today might be your opportunity to consider God's plan and purpose for your life. The reason you can praise God when you have such an opportunity is because many people do not receive the opportunity to repent of their behavior. Some die in disobedience and others live a full life, pleased with how they lived, only to find that the *cribs house* they built for themselves was worthless:[27]

Now if any man build upon this foundation gold, silver, precious stones, wood, hay, stubble; Every man's work shall be made manifest: for the day shall declare it, because it shall be revealed by fire; and the fire shall try every man's work of what sort it is. If any man's work abide which he hath built thereupon, he shall receive a reward. If any man's work shall be burned, he shall suffer loss: but he himself shall be saved; yet so as by fire.[28]

---

[26] Jonah 3:1–3.

[27] Matthew 7:21–23.

[28] 1 Corinthians 3:12–15.

Many people will stand before the Lord on the day of judgment believing they have accomplished many great works in His name. But all the hard work they spent years toiling over will be lost in moments with no reward. But you have an opportunity to change that today...

And there went great multitudes with him: and he turned, and said unto them, If any man come to me, and hate not his father, and mother, and wife, and children, and brethren, and sisters, yea, and his own life also, he cannot be my disciple. And whosoever doth not bear his cross, and come after me, cannot be my disciple. For which of you, intending to build a tower, sitteth not down first, and counteth the cost, whether he have sufficient to finish it? Lest haply, after he hath laid the foundation, and is not able to finish it, all that behold it begin to mock him, Saying, This man began to build, and was not able to finish. Or what king, going to make war against another king, sitteth not down first, and consulteth whether he be able with ten thousand to meet him that cometh against him with twenty thousand? Or else, while the other is yet a great way off, he sendeth an ambassage, and desireth conditions of peace. So likewise, whosoever he be of you that forsaketh not all that he hath, he cannot be my disciple.[29]

[29] Luke 14:25–33.

Jesus turned to the multitudes and described the requirements for being His disciple. A disciple is a student or pupil. As a student of Jesus, a disciple is to study, teach, and obey everything He commanded.[30] And to be Jesus' disciple, he or she must hate his or her:[31]

father,
mother,
wife,
children,
friends,
own life.

He or she must also bear his or her cross and follow Jesus. Carrying your cross represents following the plan and purpose God established for your life.[32]

In counting the cost of discipleship, Jesus said:[33]

For which of you, intending to build a tower, sitteth not down first, and counteth the cost, whether he have sufficient to finish it? Lest haply, after he hath laid the foundation, and is not able to finish it, all that behold

---

[30] Matthew 28:18–20.

[31] Hate in this passage is translated from the Greek as to detest or love less.

[32] Mark 14:32–42.

[33] Luke 14:28–30.

it begin to mock him, Saying, This man began to build, and was not able to finish.

A person desiring to build a tower should first consider if he or she has enough money, resources, and materials to complete the project. If he or she moves forward with the project without counting the cost, and is unable to complete the tower after laying its foundation, everyone who sees the project will mock him or her.

Counting the cost of discipleship cannot be overstated. Being a disciple of Jesus is more than attending church services, volunteering, and leading a ministry. Disciples give everything for Jesus and the kingdom of God. And you must decide whether you are willing to do the same to be His disciple.

Because many believers do not count the cost of discipleship, they find themselves as foreclosed homes, unable to provide protection, shelter, or security for themselves or those in need of Jesus. They are mocked as false representations of Christ, unable to finish the beautiful masterpiece God desired them to become. But this is not how your story has to end. *There is another way...*

Reflection

If you have been unwilling to accept God's plan and purpose for your life, how have those around you been affected by your decision?

If you were initially disobedient to God and later came to a position of godly sorrow and repentance, describe what God had to do to get your attention to change your position. Describe your actions after being brought to a *place* of godly sorrow and repentance, as well as the opportunities God allowed you to have afterward.

Have you ever counted the cost of being a disciple of Jesus? Please explain. Describe what things you would have to hate to be Jesus' disciple.

BLUEPRINTS

Except the Lord build the house, they labour in vain that build it: except the Lord keep the city, the watchman waketh but in vain.[34]

After our encounter with God, the dreams and goals we had for ourselves—even if it was something we always wanted in life—might never come to fruition. But many of those dreams and goals would not have lasted:

Love not the world, neither the things that are in the world. If any man love the world, the love of the Father is not in him. For all that is in the world, the lust of the flesh, and the lust of the eyes, and the pride of life, is not of the Father, but is of the world. And

---

[34] Psalm 127:1.

the world passeth away, and the lust thereof: but he that doeth the will of God abideth for ever.[35]

God is giving you an opportunity to receive something that will last forever. He wants you to experience His everlasting joy.[36] God wants you to willingly accept Him, believe in His Son, and fulfill the plan and purpose He has for you.

Before Jesus' betrayal and crucifixion, He did not want His disciples' hearts to be troubled. He told them to believe in God and believe in Him. Jesus wanted them to know He was preparing a place for them in His Father's house.[37]

Jesus does not want your heart to be troubled. He is also preparing a place for you in His Father's house. And as Jesus prepares a place for you in eternity, He has a blueprint for you to build a beautiful *home* through the life you live today.

God loves you so much that He gave you the opportunity to receive and share His love upon the earth. This is a part of His blueprint for your life. But your blueprint might be different from the plan and purpose God has for another person.

Consider the men and women mentioned in Hebrews 11:33–40. They were awaiting the blessed

---

[35] 1 John 2:15–17.

[36] Psalm 16:11.

[37] John 14:1–2.

entry into the eternal city, and they lived faithful lives through the blueprint God gave them. Some:[38]

subdued kingdoms,
worked out righteousness,
obtained promises,
stopped the mouths of lions,
quenched the power of fire,
escaped the edge of the sword,
from weakness grew strong,
grew mighty in war,
caused foreign armies to flee,
women received their dead by resurrection.

But there were also others who were:

tortured,
mocked and scourged,
imprisoned,
stoned,
sawn apart,
tempted,
slain with the sword,
destitute,
afflicted,
ill-treated,
wandered in deserts, mountains, caves, and the holes of the earth.

---

[38] Hebrews 11:1, 6.

But not one of them lived or died in vain. The Lord established their lives according to His good pleasure, for His glory. God provided them with a plan and purpose in this life to prepare them for an eternity with Him. They lived faithfully according to the blueprint God laid before them. They knew something so much better awaited them than what the world could give.[39] And after thousands of years, their faithful testimonies continue to speak to us.

You might not understand or see the entire blueprint God has for your life,[40] but there are three things I would like you to consider as you live for God each day:

1. No matter how bad your situation might become, God will never leave you nor forsake you.[41]

2. God will lead, guide, and instruct you through the Holy Spirit.[42]

3. The work God started in you, He will finish so you can reflect the image of Jesus on earth.[43]

---

[39] Hebrews 11:38.

[40] Isaiah 55:8–9.

[41] Psalm 23; Hebrews 13:5.

[42] John 14:16, 26, 16:6–16.

[43] Matthew 5:14–16, 43–48; John 15:1–6, Romans 8:28–29; Philippians 1:6.

Jonah experienced many hardships before accepting the blueprint God had for his life. But his story did not end with proclaiming the word of the Lord to the Ninevites or witnessing their repentance and God's removal from doing harm to them. He had but one additional lesson to learn.

Through Jonah's obedience, one hundred twenty thousand people, who did not know their right hand from their left, was spared from destruction.[44] The blueprint for Jonah's life helped to reveal the merciful hand of God, who is gracious, slow to anger, and plenteous in mercy.[45]

God does not take pleasure in the destruction of the wicked.[46] He had a blueprint of love to share with the people of Nineveh. But after the word Jonah shared with the people, his continued anger was preventing him from seeing the beauty and wonder of God's love and mercy toward them.[47]

And should not I spare Nineveh, that great city, wherein are more than sixscore thousand persons that cannot discern between their right hand and their left hand; and also much cattle?[48]

---

[44] Jonah 4:11.

[45] Psalm 103:8.

[46] Ezekiel 33:11; 1 Timothy 2:1–4; 2 Peter 3:9.

[47] Jonah 4:1–11.

[48] Jonah 4:11.

When you become discouraged, angry, and frustrated with the life God wants you to live, you lose the appreciation and awe of everything God has and is doing in your life. You lose sight of His desire to use your life to reveal His love, grace, and mercy to those who are lost and do not know their right hand from their left.[49] God wants you to be a part of the love He shares upon the earth—within you and others.

Take this time to consider the blueprint God has given you. Maybe He has not revealed the entire design of your life, but you can trust that when your building is complete, it will reflect the love and work of God.

The steps of a good man are ordered by the Lord: and he delighteth in his way. Though he fall, he shall not be utterly cast down: for the Lord upholdeth him with his hand. I have been young, and now am old; yet have I not seen the righteous forsaken, nor his seed begging bread. He is ever merciful, and lendeth; and his seed is blessed.[50]

Reflection

What areas of your blueprint has been the most challenging to complete? Please explain why.

---

[49] Mark 2:13–17.

[50] Psalms 37:23–26.

ROOMS

Like a physical house, each of us must be careful how we build on our foundation.[51] We must follow the blueprint of God's design for our lives. To follow His blueprint, there are several rooms and areas we will need to build in our lives to live faithfully unto God.

Exterior

Woe unto you, scribes and Pharisees, hypocrites! for ye are like unto whited sepulchres, which indeed appear beautiful outward, but are within full of dead men's bones, and of all uncleanness. Even so ye also outwardly appear righteous unto men, but within ye are full of hypocrisy and iniquity.[52]

---

[51] 1 Corinthians 3:10–11.

[52] Matthew 23:27–28.

In these scriptures, Jesus was calling out the scribes and Pharisees. He told them how righteous they appeared outwardly, but on the inside, were full of hypocrisy and sin. But sadly, the same can be said for many people today.

Many people place a great focus on their outward appearance and social status and standing in society and within religious groups. Like the scribes and Pharisees, they are only playing the part of a righteous person. But as believers, we must prove to be righteous through our actions.[53]

Beware of false prophets, which come to you in sheep's clothing, but inwardly they are ravening wolves. Ye shall know them by their fruits. Do men gather grapes of thorns, or figs of thistles? Even so every good tree bringeth forth good fruit; but a corrupt tree bringeth forth evil fruit. A good tree cannot bring forth evil fruit, neither can a corrupt tree bring forth good fruit.[54]

Living Room

I beseech you therefore, brethren, by the mercies of God, that ye present your bodies a living sacrifice, holy, acceptable unto God, which is your reasonable service. And be not conformed to this world: but be ye

---

[53] Matthew 15:1–20; Romans 12:1–2; Hebrews 11:1, 6.

[54] Matthew 7:15–18.

transformed by the renewing of your mind, that ye
may prove what is that good, and acceptable, and
perfect, will of God.[55]

In changing the interior of your life, you must
begin with the mind. Because we often become what
we think,[56] we must be attentive to the thoughts in
our minds.

Many of us will allow any type of thought to stay
in our minds, good or bad. Some thoughts are like
inviting robbers into your home and allowing them
to stay as long as they want. You provide them the
opportunity to roam through your house and
consider what they would like to take for themselves.
And when the opportunity comes, they will take
what they want, leaving you with the consequences.
Your thoughts work in the same way.

To transform your life, you must renew your
mind. There are three things you must do to obtain a
renewed mind:

1. Understand what keeps you conformed to this
world. Take a moment to inventory the thoughts you
had over the past week. Within the lust of the eyes
and flesh and the pride of life,[57] what kept you

---

[55] Romans 12:1–2.

[56] Proverbs 23:7.

[57] 1 John 2:15–17.

connected to the world? What things were you thinking about and meditating on that were not godly? How long did you allow negative thoughts to remain in your mind?

2. Remain watchful for negative thoughts. Just as you are careful to ensure intruders do not enter your home, you must have the same diligence for the thoughts that seek to bombard your mind.

Many of us do not want to constantly *check* for good or bad thoughts in our minds. We would much rather place our minds on *cruise control* and allow whatever thoughts come in our minds to enjoy the ride. But there is a great danger in allowing these thoughts to remain and roam free.

Consider the dialogue between Eve and the serpent.[58] Before the serpent spoke to her, she was not thinking about eating the fruit from the tree of the knowledge of good and evil. And when confronted, Eve told the serpent what God said about the fruit, "*Ye shall not eat of it, neither shall ye touch it, lest ye die.*"[59] But the serpent said that she would not die. Her eyes would be opened and would be as gods,

---

[58] Genesis 3:1–6.

[59] Genesis 3:3.

knowing good and evil.[60] Eve allowed the serpent's words to stir within her.

She looked at the tree and saw it was good for food. She looked at the tree and saw it was pleasant to the eyes. She looked at the tree and saw it was to be desired to make one wise. Eve then took its fruit and ate it, *and* gave some to her husband to eat as well.[61]

How many times has this occurred in your life? A thought—which might have *wandered* into your mind—continued to circle round and round. After a while, you saw yourself with someone you should not be with but only saw the good interactions. You saw yourself eating food you should not have but did not consider the calories afterward. You saw yourself doing things you should not do, and going places you should not go, all without thinking about the consequences of your actions.

3. Shut down negative thoughts. When you discover negative thoughts floating in your mind, you must act on them as soon as possible. The longer you allow them to remain in your mind, the greater the potential for you to act on them. So there are two courses of action you can take. The first is to pull them down.

---

[60] Genesis 3:4–5.

[61] Genesis 3:6.

Casting down imaginations, and every high thing that exalteth itself against the knowledge of God, and bringing into captivity every thought to the obedience of Christ; And having in a readiness to revenge all disobedience, when your obedience is fulfilled.[62]

Casting down these thoughts is making a decision to stop thinking about them. In one of the most impactful examples in my life, I was struggling with unforgiveness. My mind pushed my heart to continue circling around the pain this person caused and the revenge I wanted. But I knew God was telling me to just let it go and forgive. So one day I did. I decided to make a hard decision to forgive. I would let go of the painful thoughts and the revenge I sought. Right then. Right there. *And you know what?* When I made this decision, the thoughts and emotions were gone immediately.

Consider the last time something could have made you angry, and you decided not to allow it to upset you. *What happened?* Did not your mind and emotions cool down? Did not your demeanor change almost immediately? You cast down a thought and decided not to think about it.

The second course of action you can take is to answer each thought with the Word of God. The Holy Spirit led Jesus into the wilderness to be

---

[62] 2 Corinthians 10:5–6.

tempted by the devil.[63] After fasting for forty days and forty nights, Jesus was hungry. The devil said if Jesus was the Son of God, to command these stones to be made into bread.[64] Jesus responded with the Word of God:

Man shall not live by bread alone, but by every word that proceedeth out of the mouth of God.[65]

Then the devil took Jesus up into the holy city and placed Him on a pinnacle of the temple. He said if Jesus was the Son of God, He should cast Himself down, for as it is written, "*He shall give his angels charge concerning thee: and in their hands they shall bear thee up, lest at any time thou dash thy foot against a stone.*"[66] Jesus responded with the Word of God:

Thou shalt not tempt the Lord thy God.[67]

Lastly, the devil took Jesus up to a very high mountain and showed Him all the kingdoms of the world and the glory of them.[68] The devil said he

---

[63] Matthew 4:1.

[64] Matthew 4:3.

[65] Matthew 4:4.

[66] Psalm 91:11–12; Matthew 4:5–6.

[67] Matthew 4:7.

[68] Matthew 4:8.

would give all these things to Jesus if He would fall down and worship him. Jesus responded with the Word of God:

Get thee hence, Satan: for it is written, Thou shalt worship the Lord thy God, and him only shalt thou serve.[69]

After this, the devil left Jesus and angels came to minister to Him.[70]

When you submit yourself to God and resist the devil, he will flee from you.[71] But you must take an active stance against the thoughts bombarding your mind. And when you take this stance, your mind, will, and emotions will follow.

That ye put off concerning the former conversation the old man, which is corrupt according to the deceitful lusts; And be renewed in the spirit of your mind; And that ye put on the new man, which after God is created in righteousness and true holiness.[72]

---

[69] Matthew 4:10.

[70] Matthew 4:11.

[71] James 4:7.

[72] Ephesians 4:22–24.

Kitchen

For as he thinketh in his heart, so is he...[73]

When preparing any large meal, many ingredients are added to make a delicious meal. Each ingredient on its own might not create the meal you intended. It is only a single component that encompasses a larger recipe. I believe the mind and heart work in a similar manner.

When a negative thought enters your mind, your heart might take it in and provide a complementary emotion, whether it is happiness, anger, etc. By itself, that single thought might not be able to cause you to act, but some emotions can seem that strong. But what might happen if you add another thought or a different perspective of the same thought? It too is added into your *recipe*, then another emotion is tied to it...and another...and another...until you make a decision to act (good or bad).

Going back to Eve in Genesis 3:6, after the serpent spoke to her, his one statement created three separate perspectives. First, she saw that the tree was good for food—delicious. Second, she saw that the tree was pleasant to the eyes—beautiful. Third, she desired what the tree could give—wisdom. That one thought stirred her heart in three different ways, and then she

---

[73] Proverbs 23:7.

acted on what she considered—*for as she thought in her heart...*

Out of the abundance of your heart, you will speak (and act).[74] So you must not allow your heart to become troubled through your thoughts.[75] Consider these four ways to keep your heart clean:

1. Know where your heart lies.[76] The heart knows its own bitterness.[77] Even now, you know if there are things within your heart that might be keeping you from focusing on God and His Word. You might know if you are sad, angry, disappointed, depressed, etc. But even if you do, it will be good for you to take time within the next few days or week to inventory the contents of your heart. You can sit quietly before God to ask for His help in revealing everything that might be within your heart, as He knows all things and is greater than your heart.[78]

Keep your heart with all vigilance, for from it flow the springs of life.[79]

---

[74] Matthew 12:34.

[75] John 14:1.

[76] Proverbs 14:10; 1 John 3:19–20.

[77] Proverbs 14:10.

[78] 1 John 3:19–20.

[79] Proverbs 4:23.

2. Ask for help to clean your heart.[80] After King David had sex with another man's wife, had her husband killed in battle, and took her as his wife, the Lord had Nathan the prophet confront him about his sin.[81] King David later wrote a psalm describing his conduct and feelings to God. As a part of his description, he said:

Create in me a clean heart, O God; and renew a right spirit within me.[82]

To clean your heart, you must be willing to let go of what is already there. Many people want to experience a *change* in their lives but are unwilling to let go of the emotions filling their hearts. If you read Psalm 51, you will see how King David led with repentance and asked for mercy and to be cleansed of his sin. The guilt of his actions drove him to seek mercy and forgiveness from God. And with a clean heart, King David could return to living righteously before his people and God—to teach transgressors His ways and return sinners to Him.[83]

---

[80] Psalm 51:10, 86:11.

[81] 2 Samuel 11:1–27, 12:1–15.

[82] Psalm 51:10.

[83] Psalm 51:13.

This is the godly sorrow that works toward repentance to salvation.[84] This is the determination to turn from your previous thoughts and ways in sin and live righteously before God. But you must first seek to clean out everything not pleasing to the Father that is keeping you in sin.

3. Fill your mind and heart with God's Word.[85] When your heart is clean, you cannot simply wash your hands and consider the *job* done. With a clean heart, you must fill it with God's Word to keep it clean.

With my whole heart I seek you; let me not wander from your commandments! I have stored up your word in my heart, that I might not sin against you.[86]

Filling your mind and heart are intentional actions on your part. As you have one thousand four hundred forty minutes each day, you must spend as many of those minutes as you can reading, studying, and meditating on the Word of God.[87]

4. Continue to trust in God, not in yourself.[88]

---

[84] 2 Corinthians 7:10.

[85] Psalm 119:10–11; Proverbs 2:10–12, 3:3–6, 4: 23, 14:30, 17:22.

[86] Psalm 119:10–11.

[87] Joshua 1:8; Psalm 1:1–3.

[88] Proverbs 3:3–6.

Let not steadfast love and faithfulness forsake you; bind them around your neck; write them on the tablet of your heart. So you will find favor and good success in the sight of God and man. Trust in the Lord with all your heart, and do not lean on your own understanding. In all your ways acknowledge him, and he will make straight your paths.[89]

As you write steadfast love and faithfulness on the tablet of your heart, compassionate consideration and obedience to God will flow from within you.[90] And when you trust in God with all your heart and acknowledge Him, He will make your paths straight. He will place you on the road that leads to His plan and purpose—the good pleasure He has for you and others through you.

Bedrooms and Bathrooms

But thou, when thou prayest, enter into thy closet, and when thou hast shut thy door, pray to thy Father which is in secret; and thy Father which seeth in secret shall reward thee openly.[91]

The most intimate areas of a house are the bedroom and bathroom. Bedrooms often contain

---

[89] Proverbs 3:3–6.

[90] Luke 6:45.

[91] Matthew 5:6.

things that are most personal to us, yet describe our personality and what might be important to us. The most private room in the house is the bathroom. Unless you are bathing young children or you are with your spouse engaging in *extracurricular activities*, you spend your time in the bathroom alone. But more than that, these rooms provide private moments you can meet with God.

You can use these rooms to pray aloud to God and share your unfiltered thoughts. You can tell Him exactly how you might be feeling or thinking at a given moment, seek His restoration and refreshing, and unload any negative thoughts or actions through repentance or forgiveness.

Family Room, Dens, and Backyard

Family rooms, dens, and backyards are places of enjoyment with others. It is nice to be in the company of those who encourage you, help you, keep you laughing, and hold you accountable when needed.[92] But it is essential to choose your friends wisely as they can build or corrupt your character and outlook on life and God.[93]

---

[92] Proverbs 17:17, 27:6, 9, 17; Philippians 2:4.

[93] Psalm 1:1–3; Proverbs 20:19, 22:24–25, 24:21–22, 28:7, 29:3, 24; I Corinthians 15:33.

Attic and Basement

The most dangerous areas of our *house* are the attic and basement. In these areas, we place old things that we do not want to part with...things we should have thrown out years earlier. For many of us, our attic and basement represent unforgiveness, pain, and anger from our past; situations, things, and ideas we should have released to the Lord or let go of, but for many reasons, have not. And whether you realize it or not, they are often the very things that keep you from living according to God's blueprint for your life.

But there comes a time when you must clean out your attic and basement. You must go through those old memories and address the hurt and pain from your past. Only when you address your past can you accept God's plan and purpose as your own.

Do not allow negative thoughts or your past to keep you feeling bound and trapped. Many people have lived so long with their pain that they cannot see themselves living without it. They hold onto it, knowing it makes them miserable, but it is all they know. They accepted the prison of their pain and made it their own. But you must free yourself by laying aside the weights and sin that so easily entangles you.[94]

---

94 Hebrews 12:1–4.

Jesus came to set you free and give you an abundant life.[95]   God can lead you through the darkness of your valley and help you live in the light.[96] You do not have to live in bondage any longer. With God, nothing is impossible.[97]

Reflection

What *rooms* in your life require the greatest attention?

How can items in your attic and basement prevent you from living by God's plan and purpose?

Describe how you can build a home (life) where God can be glorified.

---

[95] John 8:32, 36, 10:10; Galatians 5:1.

[96] Psalm 23:4; John 3:19–21.

[97] Matthew 19:26; Luke 1:37.

DADDY'S HOUSE

When my parents divorced, I did not visit my dad's house until I was five. As I had an opportunity to visit him, I enjoyed seeing him, my Nan and Gramps, and my cousins. At the end of the week, I would often wait on the couch with my bag ready, waiting to hear his car with the diesel engine driving up the street.

Let not your heart be troubled: ye believe in God, believe also in me. In my Father's house are many mansions: if it were not so, I would have told you. I go to prepare a place for you. And if I go and prepare a place for you, I will come again, and receive you unto myself; that where I am, there ye may be also. And whither I go ye know, and the way ye know.[98]

---

[98] John 14:1–4.

Jesus is preparing a place for you. In the revelation Jesus shared with John, He provides a description of the city where His Father's house is located—the new Jerusalem.[99] It is a place of wonder and beauty.[100] God will be there to wipe away your tears, and there will be no more death, sorrow, crying, or pain.[101] They will all pass away, and you will experience the fullness of joy in His presence.[102]

From this description alone, many of us want to experience the new Jerusalem for ourselves. We would want nothing more than to have joy and peace without any thoughts of death, sorrow, crying, or pain. The description of the new city is that of a paradise made for us to enjoy with God forever.[103] And God wants you to have a place in His house. He wants everyone to have a place in His house—He wants a city filled with His creation.

The Lord is not slack concerning his promise, as some men count slackness; but is longsuffering to us-ward, not willing that any should perish, but that all should come to repentance.[104]

---

99 Revelation 1:1–2, 21:2.

100 Revelation 21:1–22:5.

101 Revelation 21:4.

102 Psalm 16:11.

103 Hebrews 11:10.

104 2 Peter 3:9.

God does not delight in the destruction of the wicked.[105] It is His desire for all people to be saved.[106] But we cannot simply walk into the new Jerusalem. As God explained to Adam, he would surely die if he ate of the fruit from the tree of the knowledge of good and evil.[107] His disobedience would not only affect him, it would affect his family and every human after him (excluding Jesus).[108]

But not as the offence, so also is the free gift. For if through the offence of one many be dead, much more the grace of God, and the gift by grace, which is by one man, Jesus Christ, hath abounded unto many. And not as it was by one that sinned, so is the gift: for the judgment was by one to condemnation, but the free gift is of many offences unto justification. For if by one man's offence death reigned by one; much more they which receive abundance of grace and of the gift of righteousness shall reign in life by one, Jesus Christ.) Therefore as by the offence of one judgment came upon all men to condemnation; even so by the righteousness of one the free gift came upon all men unto justification of life. For as by one man's disobedience

---

[105] Ezekiel 18:23, 33:11.

[106] 1 Timothy 2:3–4.

[107] Genesis 2:16–17.

[108] Romans 5:19.

many were made sinners, so by the obedience of one shall many be made righteous.[109]

God loved us so much that He sent His Son Jesus to sacrifice His life for our sins.[110] Jesus freely gave His life so that we might live with His Father for an eternity—restoring the relationship He once had with Adam and Eve. And as God reconciled us through Jesus Christ, He desires that we join Him in reconciling others to Him as well.[111]

And all things are of God, who hath reconciled us to himself by Jesus Christ, and hath given to us the ministry of reconciliation; To wit, that God was in Christ, reconciling the world unto himself, not imputing their trespasses unto them; and hath committed unto us the word of reconciliation. Now then we are ambassadors for Christ, as though God did beseech you by us: we pray you in Christ's stead, be ye reconciled to God. For he hath made him to be sin for us, who knew no sin; that we might be made the righteousness of God in him.[112]

An ambassador is an accredited diplomat sent by a country as its official representative to a foreign

---

[109] Romans 5:15–19.

[110] John 3:16–17; Romans 5:8.

[111] 2 Corinthians 5:18–21.

[112] 2 Corinthians 5:18–21.

country. Now, I would imagine being specifically called by the Most High God to be an *accredited* designation.[113] As children of God and disciples of Jesus, God desires us to go to places near and far to represent Him as witnesses.[114] As witnesses, He provides each of us with a specific plan and purpose to accomplish for Him around the world. As ambassadors of Christ, we represent Him everywhere we go, and with everyone we interact with, whether at home or school or in our work centers or local community. We are walking billboards for God, displaying who we are in Him, whether it is a good or bad representation.

Ye are the light of the world. A city that is set on an hill cannot be hid. Neither do men light a candle, and put it under a bushel, but on a candlestick; and it giveth light unto all that are in the house. Let your light so shine before men, that they may see your good works, and glorify your Father which is in heaven.[115]

If good works will glorify our Father in heaven, how do you think others will view God through our evil works? He would be put to shame.

---

[113] John 6:44; 1 Corinthians 12:3.

[114] Matthew 28:18–20; Mark 16:15; Acts 1:8.

[115] Matthew 5:14–16.

If they shall fall away, to renew them again unto repentance; seeing they crucify to themselves the Son of God afresh, and put him to an open shame.[116]

But through our love for others and good works, we have an opportunity to bring glory to God.[117] This is why you were created.[118] And as you live in this foreign country (earth), God will provide you with everything you need to be successful in being His ambassador:

Holy Spirit,[119]
talents and gifts,[120]
bible,[121]
other believers in Jesus Christ.[122]

With the blueprint God has provided for your life, there are two things I would like to remind you. First, God only has thoughts of peace for you.[123] He

---

[116] Hebrews 6:6.

[117] Proverbs 10:12; Matthew 5:14–16; John 13:34–35, 15:12; Ephesians 2:10; Hebrews 11:13–16; 1 John 4:7–12.

[118] Isaiah 43:7, 21;

[119] John 14:16–18, 26, 16:7–11, 13–14; Acts 2:16–21.

[120] Matthew 25:14–30; 1 Corinthians 12:1–11; Ephesians 4:1–16.

[121] Psalm 119:105; Jeremiah 31:31–34; Luke 11:28; 2 Timothy 3:16–17.

[122] Proverbs 27:17; Acts 14:21–22; Romans 15:1–7; Ephesians 4:29; 1 Thessalonians 5:11; Hebrews 10:23–25.

[123] Jeremiah 29:11–13.

has a future and hope for your life.[124] And sometimes, your future and hope manifest through various trials and tribulations which are used to perfect you and show others the power and glory of God:[125]

Therefore being justified by faith, we have peace with God through our Lord Jesus Christ: By whom also we have access by faith into this grace wherein we stand, and rejoice in hope of the glory of God. And not only so, but we glory in tribulations also: knowing that tribulation worketh patience; And patience, experience; and experience, hope: And hope maketh not ashamed; because the love of God is shed abroad in our hearts by the Holy Ghost which is given unto us.[126]

Second, God will not give you anything you cannot handle:

There hath no temptation taken you but such as is common to man: but God is faithful, who will not suffer you to be tempted above that ye are able; but will with the temptation also make a way to escape, that ye may be able to bear it.[127]

---

[124] Ecclesiastes 3:11.

[125] 2 Corinthians 4:1–18; Ephesians 1:19–23; James 1:1–4.

[126] Romans 5:1–5.

[127] 1 Corinthians 10:13.

There are times when many people believe what they are facing might be too much for them to handle. Things can become so difficult that they might be ready to give up and turn away from God. But nothing God does or allows is by accident. Whether you know it or not, what He has given you to do, say, or go through, He gave it to you because He knows you can accomplish it. He did not set you up to fail. God set you up to succeed and bring glory to His name.

Remember when I spoke of Gideon earlier. The reason why God wanted him to take three hundred men into battle against one hundred thirty-five thousand is that with a larger army, the people would have taken the credit for winning the battle rather than giving God the glory for helping them.[128] Sometimes, God places us in seemingly impossible situations to show His glory and power. And when you are delivered, no one can take the credit for themselves—it will all belong to God.

You are more than a conqueror through Christ! You are an overcomer![129] And those who overcome will inherit all things.[130] They will enter the new Jerusalem and live with God forever.

---

[128] Judges 7:2.

[129] John 16:33; Romans 8:31–39; 1 Corinthians 15:57; 1 John 5:4–5.

[130] Revelation 21:7.

I pray you will accept the beautiful life God has for you. He desires to spend an eternity with you and many others in perfect peace and joy. May you allow Him to build the house of your life into a beautiful representation of His love. May you fulfill the work He has given you to accomplish and receive a *well done* for your faithfulness.[131] Jesus is coming soon![132] *Amen.*

---

[131] Matthew 25:14–30.

[132] Matthew 24:36–51; Revelation 22:7–21.

(com)mission™

P U B L I S H I N G

www.commissionpubs.com
info@commissionpubs.com

www.ingramcontent.com/pod-product-compliance
Lightning Source LLC
Chambersburg PA
CBHW071640040426
42452CB00009B/1709